His smile grew enormous. "I've gotten so much. Even my blindness . . . it has helped to intensify the whole experience of life. Till my dying day I'll try to give of myself, of the love I've been given so much of. I'll try to give love and peace, the inner peace I've won . . . the positive thoughts . . . I'll give to anyone around.

"I want to play and sing for people. And I want to give of the money that keeps coming in. Such a lot of money. Never did I think I'd meet such appreciation from my fellow humans.

"You know, nothing's ever promised to us in this world. Just being able to breathe is a gift from God. Then one has to shape and form one's life with what one has. And if things go well, then it's necessary, absolutely necessary, to share some of this. If one gets rich, why not give to those who have nothing?"

STEVIE WONDER

by MARIANNE RUUTH

AN ORIGINAL HOLLOWAY HOUSE EDITION
HOLLOWAY HOUSE PUBLISHING CO.
LOS ANGELES, CALIFORNIA

PUBLISHED BY
Holloway House Publishing Company
8060 Melrose Avenue
Los Angeles, California 90046
International Standard Book Number 0-87067-315-7
Printed in the United States of America
Cover illustration by Bryant Eastman
Cover design by Davidson Graphics

CHAPTER ONE

Monday, August 6, 1973 . . .

The scene is a highway near Salisbury, North Carolina.

A rented car is moving along. It comes from Greenville, South Carolina. Its destination is Durham, North Carolina, specifically Duke University, where big posters proclaim BENEFIT CONCERT ... STEVIE WONDER ... IN PERSON!

Twenty-three-year-old Stevie Wonder

himself is sound asleep in the front passenger seat. Yes, he's wearing a seat belt. In the driver's seat is his cousin, John Wesley Harris—he and Stevie grew up together in Detroit.

Ahead of the car is a large flatbed truck, hauling logs.

Everything happens fast, too fast.

The logging truck driver either slows down or comes to a stop, causing Harris to swerve in an attempt to pass. The right side of the car fails to clear the truck. There is the sound of metal hitting metal, the awful screeching of brakes. A chain breaks loose . . .

A huge log comes hurtling at the car.

Twisted chrome and metal, a shattered windshield—the log slams right into Stevie Wonder's forehead.

In the wrecked car. Stevie Wonder lies motionless. Unconscious. Covered with blood.

He is pried from the wreck and taken to North Carolina Baptist Hospital. He is admitted at 9:05 p.m. "All his vital signs are stable," it is reported, but he is in intensive care, and he remains in a coma.

Harris, also injured in the crash, is listed in good condition.

Stevie is not going to come out of the coma for four long days. The doctors diagnose his injuries as a fractured skull and a brain contusion (a severe bruise of brain tissue).

Will he make it? Will he ever sing again?

6

Ever make music again? Is he ever going to say, "Man, am I glad just to be alive!" moving his head back and forth and sideways as he has a habit of doing when he feels good?

Those are the anguished questions of relatives, friends, and fans, near and far.

Rumors are going to fly for weeks ... rumors concerning permanent brain damage. It is told "as fact" that Stevie will never be the same again, that he'll be a vegetable. It is repeated that the doctors at the hospital said that, because Stevie is blind, the impact of the accident was magnified three times.

But his name isn't Wonder for nothing, and when it comes to stubborn strength and willpower and burning desire to live and live fully, few can match him.

His friend and aide since around 1968, Ira Tucker, Jr., could usually be found at Stevie's bedside. In an interview shortly after the accident, Tucker described what it was like at the hospital in Winston-Salem.

"Man, I couldn't even recognize him. His head was swollen up about five times normal size. And nobody could get through to him."

Tucker tried talking to Stevie, tried shouting in his ear, tried everything he could think of. No reaction.

Then one day he thought he saw the slightest sign of Stevie regaining consciousness. Ira knelt down, leaned over, put his mouth close to Stevie's ear and began to sing some

7

lines from "Higher Ground," Stevie's song (released a week before the accident) about getting a second chance.

Stevie's hand was resting on Ira's arm and suddenly his fingers started going with the song, moving to the music.

A smile split Ira's worried face. "I said, yeah! This dude is gonna make it!"

The news was told, no *shouted* to all those who had been thinking of Stevie Wonder, praying for him, hoping, doubting, fearing: Stevie was not going to die. He was going to live!

But would he sing again? Would he be the same?

Maybe nobody is the same after a close brush with death.

When he came to, his sense of smell was completely gone, and it was thought at first that the damage might be permanent. But Stevie responded beautifully to treatment, and, as he healed, his sense of smell returned.

In another interview, Ira Tucker insisted that he knew Stevie would be fully recovered when he began grabbing the nurses at the hospital. "That's when I knew that he was gonna be the same as ever. Soon as I knew he was thinking about going after women again, I knew he was on the road to recovery."

Jokes were flying between Stevie and his friends during the long weeks in the hospital (after two weeks, he was brought to UCLA

Medical Center in Los Angeles). His sense of humor had remained intact, that was obvious. But the jokes were just a thin surface covering a distinct fear: Could his ability to make music – this hard-to-define, special, personal magical talent of his – have been wiped out by the impact of the log? What is artistic talent anyway? Where is it located? How is it born, and how does it grow? The music *is* Stevie Wonder; his music is the man he is. What would he be without it. Truly handicapped for the first time in his life?

For his blindness is not a handicap, he has refused to let it become so. He is sightless, yes, but blind? No! Handicapped? No way!!

The day arrived when his friends brought an instrument, a clavinet, to the hospital room. Stevie fell silent. Nobody else said a word either. The fear in that room was almost physical. Then, slowly, Stevie reached out, touched it, let his fingers feel its shape, its presence. Some notes escaped, hesitantly at first, then with jubilant surety the music was born.

Stevie Wonder was not permanently damaged by the accident that so easily could have killed him. Instead, this close contact with death signaled a new phase of his life, a more intense and creative phase than before. More intense. That says a lot since so much had happened already during his twenty-three years on this planet.

His first American concert after the accident was in New York's Madison Square

Garden. A big angry pink splotch of a scar showed about his familiar dark glasses. He was sporting a mustache.

He walked onto the stage, he pointed toward heaven, he pointed to his forehead. He smiled, a survivor's smile.

Twenty thousand voices broke into a roar of adulation, welcome, and pure joy.

Then began that exchange between performer and audience that is so typical of Stevie Wonder, the communication and inspiration and response, the magical Wonder tour.

That whole summer preceding the accident, the summer of 1973, Stevie had been carrying around strange premonitions. He kept having an uneasy feeling that something was going to happen to him. He didn't know what that something was. He only knew, somehow, that it would mean a big change in his life.

That was the summer his album *Innervisions* was released.

Like all his works, *Innervisions* reveals a lot about Stevie and his feelings regarding a great number of things.

"Too High" reflects crazy joy, and, in the middle of it, there is the line, "I feel like I'm about to die."

"Visions" expresses Stevie's visions of the world as it ought to be. He is a realist, he knows what exists, but he keeps seeing this vision of people living "hand in hand," of a world where hate is a disappearing dream, and love reigns supreme.

"Living for the City" lets us feel the gnawing frustrations of living in a big city ghetto.

"Golden Lady" is about the love he's ready to dare again.

And "Higher Ground," the song that would bring him back to life, is an almost prophetic proclamation about getting a second try at life, at a life that is going to be *more*, that's going to mean more, that's going to be lived on "higher ground." Clayton Riley in the *New York Times* called that specific song, written several months before the accident, "a portrait of initial gloom that climbs to righteous affirmation. A strange song, mystery all around it."

"Jesus Children of America" is about the Jesus movement and asks how real is the so-called spiritual awakening happening all around?

"All in Love Is Fair," "Don't You Worry 'Bout A Thing," "He's Misstra Know It All," show a strong sense of life, a keen understanding of what's going on, and his ability to *see* more than most of us.

The music and the lyrics fit together like hand in glove, float through the air and into our minds. Stevie throws us inspiration for a better world, a richer, fuller, finer life. But, at the same time, he's fully aware of our shortcomings. Is all this possible? he asks. Can we do it? If we try, together?

His music paints his portrait: A man who sees clearly and reacts directly to the world around him. That is Stevie Wonder, blind from birth, black and beautiful, raised in a teeming, smoky industrial ghetto, in a broken home, not being born with any silver spoon in his mouth but growing golden ideas in his head. A *super star*, nationally and internationally acclaimed.

Even reviewers grow poetic at times. The weirdly prophetic *Innervisions* received glowing reviews. Clayton Riley in the *New York Times* kept calling Stevie "The Wonder" and said that he "identifies himself as a gang and a genius, producing, composing, arranging, singing, and, on several tracks, playing all the accompanying instruments (yes, it is impossible, or used to be). But Stevie Wonder, you see, wants to know more. *More*. At the center of his music is the sound of what is real. Vocally, he remains inventive and unafraid, he sings all the things he hears: rock, folk, and all forms of black music. The sum total of these varying components is an awesome knowledge, consumed and then shared by an artist who is free enough to do both."

Talented songbird Roberta Flack said of Stevie's music, "It's the most sensitive of our decade . . . he has tapped the pulse of the people . . ."

As Stevie's family and the world celebrated his survival and recovery, many wondered about his strange premonitions. He said in an interview in *Rolling Stone* the spring before his accident, "Sometimes I have dreams. Sometimes I feel that certain things are gonna happen. I had a dream about Benny Benjamin (Motown's studio drummer who died in 1969 of a stroke). I talked to him a few days before he died; he was in the hospital. But in my dream I talked to him, he said, 'Look man, I'm . . . I'm not gonna make it . . . ' 'What, you kiddin'?' The image . . . he was sitting on my knee, which seems like he was very weak. And he said, 'So, like I'm leavin' it up to you.' That was like a Wednesday and that following Sunday I went to church and then to the studio to do a session: we were gonna record 'You Can't Judge a Book By Its Cover' and they said, 'Hey, man, we're not gonna do it today, Benny just died.' "

Premonitions, forewarnings. Is Stevie Wonder more sensitive to such things, does he voyage through "X" dimensions? Did this sensitivity increase after the accident? Some believe that. Obvious to all is that there is a quality about his music that gives it a metaphysical tint. It's sometimes as if it were lifted out of ordinary time and space, as if it were nearer to some kind of cosmic awareness.

At one time, Stevie told *Crawdaddy Magazine*: "I would like to believe in reincarnation. I would like to believe that there is another life. I think that sometimes your consciousness can happen on this earth a second time around. For me, I wrote 'Higher Ground' even before the accident. But something must have been telling me that something was going to happen to make me aware of a lot of things and to get *myself* together. This is like my second chance for life, to do something or to do more, and to value the fact that I am alive."

In response to the interviewer's question if he felt at any time that he had left his body, Stevie said, "I did feel that way. I know that I possibly did but I don't know where I went . . . because what happened to me was a very, very critical thing and I was really supposed to die."

Yet another time he told Henry Edwards of *New York Magazine*, "The only thing I know about it is what I read. I was asleep when it happened, so I can't tell you what happened. Then I was out for days so I can't tell you about that either."

He told an interviewer in *People* 1976: "It was God tellin' me it was time I figured out who and where my friends were. Life has to be positive – we learn from experience. Gotta keep rollin' forward, not rewind."

And hear what a press release declared: "While outwardly it appeared that he was unconscious, inwardly the furiousness of his awareness, perception, and determination were accelerating at breakneck speed. It was during this time that the sublime became the reality of the innermost visions of the man, and that the concepts so eloquently stated throughout his then most recent work, *Innervisions* – particularly 'Higher

Ground'—were truly fulfilled."

Whew, high-sounding words that, but we often reach for such when we, maybe with a shiver along the spine, try to understand what it means to be near death, that big unknown. Stevie himself avoids the big words. He expresses thanks that he was allowed to live a bit longer, and he seems to know what he's going to do with life. *Life*—the word is real to him. He is determined to do his part to help to give birth to a new world. As if he sees a new kind of human being in the bud, and wants to brings such a being to flamboyant flower. In a climate of love, he seems to say, we humans may grow and flower together. There's a oneness to life. We are different but all the same.

It would be fun to spend hours, days, weeks, just talking to Stevie Wonder, to ask him all kinds of nosy questions. But one senses a reluctance in him. Altogether, he has not given many interviews. What he has to say, what he believes and wishes to communicate, all comes out in his music. His whole life story is there. His records (from *Music of My Mind* and on) come with lyrics included so that we may sing along, may learn by heart (literally) and absorb his messages. His songs have to do with a nucleus, center of things, heart of the matter. He is very, very sharp and very, very alert. This was evident before the accident, but it's crystal-clear afterwards.

Physically, it took Stevie some time to get

15

his strength back. But, by winter, he was strong enough for a concert tour in Europe. He played in Cannes, France to sold-out houses. He went to England, and his success was great. His former road manager, Ira Siddelle, commented, "The kid's an international hero. Over in England, he's just like Babe Ruth. They all stop him on the street."

HERE COME THE GRAMMIES ... WATCH OUT! Every year, the American music industry honors its artists of the past year. So it did in March, 1974. The National Academy of Recording Arts & Sciences voted and handed out the much sought-after Grammy awards. Stevie Wonder was highly visible as he won award after award. Some newspapers rechristened them "The Stevie Wonder Awards."

First he won a Grammy for Best Rhythm and Blues Song of the Year and promptly gave it to his mother, Lula Mae Hardaway, who came up on the stage, nearly bursting with pride and emotion, and received it from his hand.

The awards kept coming after that.

He won for Best Rhythm and Blues Vocal Performance ("Superstition"), Best Pop Vocal Performance ("You Are the Sunshine of My Life"), and Album of the Year (*Innervisions*). This album also won a Grammy as Best Engineered Recording of the Year.

Not quite twenty-four-years-old—and he had 20 hit singles, 15 best-selling albums and *five* Grammy Awards in one year! This had never happened to a single artist before.

Stevie Wonder was definitely recognized as one of the major talents on the contemporary music scene.

Now he could take it easy, rest on his triumphs, bask in the sunshine of fame. Could—but wouldn't. He was eager to go on to new things, new discoveries. The closeness to death had its effect.

"You begin to really value time, and realize the importance of doing what you have to do in as much time as you have, 'cause tomorrow is not promised to any of us," he said.

Friends comment on the changes in him brought about by the accident. "That accident changed him more than anything else," is an often-heard observation. He used to be more restless, used to call friends at four in the morning and want to work or talk or do something. After the accident, he seemed to know more what it was all about. He remained as busy—or even busier than ever—but no longer was he in the grip of *feverish* activity. It was as if he knew now what he was required to do.

He decided that 1974 would end one era in his career, the era that had started when he signed his first contract with Motown at the age of ten, when he became Little Stevie Wonder rather than Steveland Morris and was hailed as Hitsville's "12-Year Old Genius," the Wonder boy.

There are different eras, different levels, throughout Stevie Wonder's life. At ten, he stepped out of being just another little blind boy and began a professional life. He was so young, and he was blind. Motown became his father substitute, his legal guardian, overseer of his education. Motown employed tutors who emphasized hard work and discipline. The goal was perfection. Motown booked his concerts and guided his career. Young and old adored that cute little boy. Everybody was impressed by his unique musicality, unfailing sense of rhythm and endless inventiveness, as well as his uncommon and often loudly expressed joy at being alive and being allowed to live in a world of music.

"The music is a world in itself." He has said that many times, never quite understanding why people want to know so much about him personally. Wasn't his music enough?

He grew up, turned twenty-one and felt a need for change. His music matured with him. He rebelled against Motown, demanded total artistic freedom – and got it.

He invented complex new musical textures, using the Moog and Arp synthesizers. He went on tour with the Rolling Stones, thereby capturing a massive white audience as well, as he was exposed to them and they to him.

At the age of twenty-three, at the time of the accident, Stevie Wonder was on top. After the accident, he climbed even higher.

His caring for others became intensified. He doesn't talk about what he does charity-wise. He becomes generally edgy when people talk about money. "Of course, he set up his mother and the younger kids in a big house in California," one friend says. "He has helped a lot of other relatives, childhood buddies, and fellow artists . . . and there's more than one minority business that got started with a little help from friend Stevie . . ."

That spring of 1974, he said his thanks to life by a special American concert tour to raise money for charities. He declared that he wanted to divide his donations between organizations in the United States and in Africa.

His share of the profits from the tour's opening concert at Madison Square Garden was $34,000. Every penny of it went to a program providing summer recreation facilities for inner-city children.

In all he did, one could sense that he was looking forward, that his horizons were expanding.

"I have to always evolve and move ahead and express to the world things that I see that people don't see; things that I feel that people don't take the time to feel; sounds that people ignore and don't hear."

On March 14, 1974, he held a press conference at Century Plaza in Los Angeles.

Now, professional writers don't go to press conferences expecting to cry. Journalists

19

tend to become slightly cynical. They have heard the big words, the expansive promises, have see the big gestures before. They tend to look for flaws in the presented image. They are wary of sounding like press releases in their own writing, of presenting anyone interviewed and written about as a knight in shining armor, a perfect example of a perfect or nearly perfect human being. "Show the warts," editors keep hollering at their staff. "Idols have feet of clay."

But that sunny day in March, there were tears, more or less hidden, in many a journalistic eye. The whole thing was so different from a regular press conference. ("Meet Mr. Wonderful – or Miss Wonderful! Isn't she/he fantastic, the living end?! Just don't ask about that beating, that rap, that smelly divorce, that piece of rumor," press representatives caution in buttery voices.)

This was a different experience. No press agents visible anywhere.

"I came here to tell you of my appreciation for all you've done for me," Stevie began sincerely.

Still twenty-three-years-old, having won a record number of Grammy awards, obviously being enormously talented, he sat there with eyes moving unseeingly behind dark glasses and spoke in a low, gentle voice, sometimes falteringly, about what he was going to do and what he believed in.

"I believe in giving – but I keep receiving more than I give," he said.

"Actions speak louder than words. I want to do more for children. That's a worthwhile thing for all of us to do. The children . . . they're our future – they need education and love, those basic things in life . . ."

He told how he in the months following the accident made a decision: to leave and go to live in Ghana, Africa, in approximately two years.

"I love *this* country. I'm not saying goodbye. To leave, to go, to learn something is a beginning. I will keep up my music. I will come back often. I will keep on with my concerts, my records. But when you get as close to death as I did a few months ago," he said and touched the scars on his right temple, "then there's a definite change in you. I got time to think in the hospital, about me and the world. Today is not yesterday . . .

"I'm grateful to the people in America . . . they have made Stevie Wonder out of Steveland Morris . . . they have let me go on, they've given me the freedom to create my music as I feel it. To do my thing. To sing my songs . . .

"If I can do a concert . . . stand there on the stage and do what I like best . . . and because of that kids in a ghetto can get away from the unhealthy things, from the hopelessness . . . and spend a summer in God's nature . . . then I'm blessed . . . and grateful.

"I don't want to be a star! What is that? What does it mean? What do I care about riding in a Cadillac! It's what you are inside

21

that's important, that's the only thing that's important."

Simply but strongly, he told how he wanted to help people in Ghana, children and adults. "Seventy-five percent of the people there are blind! There are fungus-carrying flies, millions of flies . . . they get into the eyes and literally eat the cornea."

He spoke about deprived African children, about all the existing great needs, not taken care of by the countries themselves.

It was absolutely quiet in the room. Stevie's honesty was evident, his charisma obvious. There's something magnetic about him, about that voice, the words he says. You're spellbound, you listen.

He is the same as his songs. There are the same strong feelings put into words, into music – you have to listen. You are touched deep inside – that secret, protected inside that some call the soul. And you feel an urge, maybe only momentarily, to be a little bit better in your everyday life, to really *see* what's important and *do* something.

"Life's not about the glitter, the clothes, the money," he said with quiet intensity. "Life is about sharing, about giving with joy and love without expecting things in return. That's the problem. Too many give and expect something back. That's no good. Just give."

His smile grew enormous. "I've gotten so much. Even my blindness . . . it has helped to intensify the whole experience of life. Till my dying day I'll try to give of myself, of the love I've been given so much of. I'll try to give love and peace, the inner peace I've won . . . the positive thoughts . . . I'll give to anyone around.

"I want to play and sing for people. And I want to give of the money that keeps coming in. Such a lot of money. Never did I think I'd meet such appreciation from my fellow humans.

"You know, nothing's ever promised to us in this world. Just being able to breathe is a gift from God. Then one has to shape and form one's life with what one has. And if things go well, then it's necessary, absolutely necessary, to share some of this. If one gets rich, why not give to those who have nothing?"

So spoke Stevie Wonder, a guy who knows the score – in more ways than one. Every word grew from a conviction that he lives out. Later on, he changed his plans to move to Ghana for a number of reasons. He remains living in America but his caring and his giving, both here and there, go on.

People are forever calling him miraculous and at the same time trying to explain, analyze, and define him and his music. Define Stevie? It reminds one of when Louis Armstrong was asked for a definition of jazz and supposedly answered something to the effect: "If y'gotta ask, ya'll never know."

He is whatever you experience in his music. It would be easy to apply adjective after adjective to Stevie, but how many times can one say fresh, inspired, and beautiful without sounding like a commercial for cake frosting?

So let's mention instead his crazy sense of humor. How he tosses a joke into the middle of a serious discussion, how good he is at mimicking somebody, anybody, how he has a knack for coming up with something unexpected.

There was the time, 1968 or so, when he made an album called *Eivets Rednow*. Yes, that's right, that's *Stevie Wonder* spelled backwards!

Some people got the joke right away. Others didn't.

It happened in a crowded airport that a man came up to Stevie with concern written all over his face. "Hey, man, Stevie, those whites are takin' over everything. Look, I heard a kid today, man, played 'Alfie' just like you, man!"

"Oh yeah, this cat named Rednow?" Stevie said. "Don't worry 'bout him!"

There's a lot of laughter in Stevie, and maybe, just maybe, a person's sanity can be measured by the person's ability to laugh.

A survivor with a huge smile, that's Stevie Wonder. He has survived blindness, poverty, broken home, early stardom, advice from experts, a broken heart (more than once), the lure of fame, being a millionaire. He's a survivor all right. Death didn't claim him that autumn day in 1973 either. If his life had been meant to be brief, that would have been it, is the feeling of many.

CHAPTER TWO

Each century is conveniently sliced into decades, and each decade seems to have a mood, a feeling all its own. There was the '40s, with war tearing the world apart, the slow healing, the birth of hope. The '50s was characterized by longings and frustrations, a certain tremulous insecurity in Western society. One could see the signs that led to the consciousness, the awareness of the '60s, the Vietnam era, the social upheaval. Then came the introspective '70s.

The '50s was James Dean in "East of Eden" and Harry Belafonte singing calypso. The '60s was Bob Dylan, James Brown, the Beatles, Sidney Poitier in "In the Heat of the Night" and Dick Gregory in jail.

As the '50s had just tiptoed in, before that decade's "silent generation" knew what was happening, Stevie Wonder made his entrance into our world.

It happened in Saginaw, Michigan, a city (population in 1950 was 92,918) situated on both sides of the Saginaw River. This used to be Indian country. Indian trails crossed at Saginaw, and many Indian villages were in the vicinity. Lewis Cass negotiated a treaty in 1819 with the Indians, who ceded much of Michigan to the United States. Saginaw is a port of entry and an industrial center surrounded by an agricultural area.

Saginaw was where a baby boy was born on May 13, 1950.

He was the third in a poor family of six children, not all having the same father.

Stevie's own father wasn't around much nor too long, though he made Stevie feel special by telling him that Saginaw was twelve miles from the North Pole. For a long time, Stevie believed this, and he and his older brother Calvin used to go around telling everybody that they were born twelve miles from the North Pole.

He was born Steveland Judkins—Judkins was his biological father's name. Then his mother, a capable, loving woman named Lula Mae, moved the family 96 miles southeast to Detroit where he grew up as Steveland Morris. Morris was his first stepfather's name. Later on, he would have another stepfather whose name was Hardaway. A lot of names to choose from for a boy who would become Stevie Wonder. To further confuse the issue, when he filed a suit in 1976 in connection with his car accident, his actual name was given as Steven Douglas Morris. And sometimes he signs his name (as on the album *The Secret Life of Plants*) as Steveland Morris. Well, what's in a name? A Wonder by any other name would still be a Wonder, right?

But let's get back to the poor, black boy living in the ghetto on the east side of Detroit. In "upper-lower-class circumstances," as he himself puts it.

He was born blind. He was the only one of the six children born with a handicap. Possibly the reason for his blindness is that he was born a full month prematurely. There is a theory that the reason more specifically may be exposure to too much oxygen during his long stay in the incubator. (There is a dislocated nerve in one eye, a cataract in the other.)

Stevie first became aware of being blind when he was playing out in the back of the house and kept getting into dog manure. His mother told him that he shouldn't move around so much but try to stay more in one place. This he found extremely difficult (and still does).

Being blind was, of course, normal to him. But he knew that it worried his mother, and that she prayed for him to have sight some day.

She also used to take him to various faith healers to "cure" his blindness. He was chanted over, prayed over, hands were laid upon him. Congenital blindness was regarded as a disease by those around him. But he never believed it was a disease, never accepted it as a real handicap.

One day, the little boy went to his mother and told her that he was *happy* being blind, that he thought it was a gift from God. She seemed to feel better after that.

He was not treated with cotton gloves because he was blind. Sometimes he got whipped—with the ironing cord. The Magic Iron Cord Whipping as he remembers it. But then, by his own admission, he was pretty wild at times. There were small wooden sheds in back of the houses on the street where he lived. The neighborhood kids would hop from one to another, and Stevie was one of these kids.

But, how could he? Being blind.

There's a wonderful law of compensation at work. Blind people tend to develop their other senses to an extreme degree at an early age. Stevie wasn't very old when he could tell birds apart by their different calls and songs. Even trees sounded different to him when the wind blew through their leaves. He learned to hear how sound *bounces off* objects, how if he called out something, he could tell if he was close or far away from an object. Such as the roof of a shed (a holler, cocked head while he listened to a faint echo, then off he went in a precision jump).

Fine and dandy, but what would the future have to offer this poor, blind boy? It seemed likely that Steveland Morris from Detroit's public projects would end up somewhere making brooms or standing on street corners selling pencils.

Except for one thing. This boy, coming from a not especially musical family (though his mother was a gospel singer for awhile) had a special one-to-one relationship with music. This was evident at an early age. The story has been told many times how he, at the tender age of two, sat and pounded a tin pan with a spoon to the rhythm of the music on the radio.

Since he experienced much of the world around through his ears, music became his greatest delight. He listened intently to all sounds. He heard voices, heard how they were different, how much they told him about people. He listened to screams and laughter. Cars rolling by, airplanes zooming overhead. Bark and whine of dogs, crickets with their peculiar song-producing organs on the front wings. Wind, falling rain, rustling leaves. Isolated footsteps on pavement. In church there was gospel music, and on the radio there was rhythm and blues to fill his being. He seemed to be always listening, keeping time with what he heard, moving his head and his body to the music.

One day he and his family had a picnic in a park where a band was playing. Stevie bounced and rocked to the rhythm, banged two spoons together, intent on the sounds streaming toward him. The drummer in the band noticed the small boy, became fascinated by him, went over and asked if he'd like to try playing the drums. Stevie smiled his big smile. He was too small even to reach the drums, but the drummer took him on his lap and Stevie played. People gathered around, listened, marvelled, applauded – and Stevie heard the sound of coins being thrown on the stage.

He could probably tell exactly where they were, too. There was a game people played with him from the age of four or five. "What is it, Stevie?" they would ask as they threw a coin on the kitchen table.

He always had an answer right away. "Dime . . . nickel . . . quarter . . . " whatever it was. He nearly always got the coins right, except that the sound of a penny and that of a nickel confused him sometimes.

After the picnic and the drum playing, his folks knew what to give him for Christmas: a set of toy drums, the dime store kind with cardboard tops. They had to be replaced quite often for he banged them so hard that there was no way they could last from Christmas to Christmas.

His first real musical instrument was a harmonica that a barber who had noticed his love for music gave him when he was five. He taught himself to play it. It was a four hole model that Stevie wore on a chain around his neck. Shortly after entering school, he was given a small radio of his own. He also began to teach himself to play piano. He was about nine when he began to pick out tunes on a neighbor's piano. He loved it so intently that the neighbor gave him the piano when she moved. At that time, he also received his first real drum, a snare drum, as part of the Detroit Lions Club's donations to blind children.

Stevie took special classes for the blind in Detroit's public school system. He learned to speak clearly and to show facial expressions—being blind, he had never seen how people move their lips or their faces. He learned how to use his hearing even more efficiently, how all sounds echo against things around. He learned to use his touch, how to feel changes in the air against his skin. He also learned Braille, the system of writing or printing for the blind, in which combinations of raised dots represent letters of the alphabet.

At around eight or nine, he began going out by himself, though there was usually a sighted person with him. He has said that he rarely ended up in situations where he was scared or felt alone.

Though, of course, it happened. There was the time when he went to stay with his father – after his parents had broken up. His father, who seems to have had a lively imagination, promised him candy and bubblegum and rides on a bus. Stevie was excited. At his father's place, there was a piano and a saxophone, an instrument he never had touched before. Stevie stayed there for a while. But then, one day the father went off somewhere and stayed away for what seemed like a long time. "That was the first time I got upset," Stevie said in an interview. He cried himself to sleep. But who does he blame? Not his father but the unfamiliar surroundings.

Fear, loneliness, bitterness, anger – it was all dispelled by music. Music became a kind of inner home. Music gave him warmth and joy. He spent hours and hours just listening to the radio. He began to know different instruments intimately. His favorite radio program was called *Sundown*. There he heard Johnny Ace, Jimmy Reed, Mavis Staples. He became enthralled by the then relatively new rhythm and blues, particularly as B.B. King would sing it.

He seems to have rejected pity at a very early age, from strangers as well as from his own family. His mother encouraged his reliance on himself. Though he remembers wryly once when he was very small and his not too much older brothers Milton and Calvin were talking about him, feeling sorry for him. Stevie needs more light, then maybe he can see, the two boys concluded. They wanted to give their brother more light. They collected all kinds of stuff, put it inside a garbage can and set fire to it, thereby nearly setting the house on fire.

He was a wiry kid who could climb any tree the other kids could climb, a mischievous boy who discovered the niceness of girls at an early age and liked to play doctor (as he reveals in a song). He loved to ride the bicycle (with someone, usually his brother Calvin, sitting behind him to steer). He was determined to lead a normal life. He ran fast, he could catch things he threw into the air. He let his hearing and his sensitive touch guide him. The more he attempted, the more he could do.

He was named a junior deacon at the Whitestone Baptist Church in Detroit, he sang in the church choir, and he often was asked to sing solo at the services. Sometimes he thought it would be nice to become a minister.

Music was the biggest part of his life. As he kept listening, he kept making his own music. He and some friends used to play for the whole neighborhood on front porches of the houses on Horton Street. The crowds got bigger, the musicians grew more confident, the music became more intense. Wilder, some said. Then one day, during a particularly inspired, ear-splitting session on a front porch, one lady from the church the family attended happened to walk by. She stopped in shock. She recognized Stevie and exclaimed in a loud voice, "I'm ashamed of you, Stevie, for playing that worldly music out here. I'm ashamed of you!"

The word was spread, others reacted, and so it happened that Stevie Wonder, at nine years of age, was kicked out of the church choir and of being a deacon because he was singing rock'n'roll. "And that's how I became a sinner," he jokes.

He kept being filled with blues and jazz and all else he heard. He imitated different aspects of music. He loved the way Jackie Wilson sang rhythm and blues, but he began to love one singer above all others. Ray Charles, perhaps the greatest pop singer of his generation, the man who has composed and performed some of the most influential and lasting records of the rock'n'roll era, who has fused gospel and blues and southwestern jazz into a special soul-searching music, became Stevie's idol above all others. Ray Charles is twenty years older than Stevie Wonder. He is also blind (by glaucoma when he was six) but maybe that was not the only thing with which Stevie Wonder identified. One senses a likeness of attitude in these two singers. "I never wanted to be famous, but I always wanted to be great," Ray Charles has said. These words could have been uttered by Stevie Wonder.

Young Stevie heard saxophonists such as

King Curtis and attempted to imitate those sounds on his harmonica.

He kept playing or attempting to play more instruments: piano, drums, harmonica, plus bongos . . . and hookey, he would probably add with a grin.

In his neighborhood, the youngster's exceptional music talent was recognized, even if everybody didn't approve, understand, or couldn't bear rattling window panes!

In that neighborhood lived a family named White. One of the younger boys was a friend of a friend of Stevie's and that's how it happened that an older boy, Ronnie White, came to hear Stevie. Ronnie was a singer in the rhythm and blues group *The Miracles*. He listened to the ten-year-old Stevie playing harmonica and singing and was impressed. So impressed, in fact, that he arranged an audition for Stevie at *The Miracles'* recording company, then called Hitsville. Four years later the name of the company was changed to Motown, simply a contraction of Motor Town, which was what blacks in Detroit called the automobile capital.

This, by the way, is something of a tradition at Motown, that one artist discovers and brings in others. Diana Ross was the one who discovered the Jackson Five and brought that group to the company.

Stevie went to the audition. He sang and played some standard blues plus a few songs he himself had written. (The first song he wrote at ten was "Lonely Boy." It was about a girl – of course.)

"I wasn't shy," he recalls happily. "I opened up."

A Motown mogul puts it this way, "He came up here and we never let him go!"

The president of the company is Berry Gordy Jr., a young songwriter who had been encouraged by Smokey Robinson to start an all-black label. (Smokey Robinson also grew up in the Detroit ghetto – so did Diana Ross, two of the Temptations, Aretha Franklin and all Four Tops. Could it be the air?) Berry Gordy Jr. knew a talent when he heard it, and he didn't hesitate to present Stevie with a five year recording contract. Of course, the contract had to be signed by Stevie's mother since he was so young.

Not long afterwards, the boy wonder was handed a new name to go with his new life: Little Stevie Wonder.

There's a quote from Stevie about that time, a small boy with a smiling face: "I'd like to buy my mother a home, and some instruments so I can play at home. Berry is going to give me a tape recorder."

As an adult he commented, "I was just another little blind boy before I came to Hitsville. That was the best thing that ever happened to me."

The only thing he wasn't crazy about was his new name. A couple of times later, he would contemplate changing it back to Steveland Morris.

The '50s for Stevie Wonder were his first ten years of life, ten years as a poor boy from a broken home. His mother did her best, but her best was only so much.

The '60s meant he was a professional with a contract. The best things about that, he discovered, was having more money, more clothes, and more food than ever before. He also liked having more attention, often a scarce commodity in a large family.

Every day, after school, Stevie went to Hitsville. He played every instrument, he basked in the attention he was given. Slowly, he learned the "Hitsville sound." Most songs, he found, were about love, and they were easy to dance to.

"He was a pest. All those questions—he never gave up. But he was a talented pest," studio musicians remember.

In school, Stevie continued to do well and kept up a solid B average. But some people at school were skeptical about his sudden career. He was too young, they reasoned. It was happening too fast. It would ruin him for life, would make him expect things that don't happen to people like him. Like so many, they had trouble believing that somebody they knew well and saw every day could actually make it.

Late at night, when all was quiet, Stevie often read to his brothers from his Bible. All in Braille, of course. He liked the sounds of the words, many of the thoughts, and he liked reading aloud. Voices fascinated him

38

more and more, including his own voice.

On weekends, he played concerts.

At Hitsville/Motown, his financial affairs were carefully watched. Some earnings went to his family to cover his expenses at home. The rest went into a trust fund that would make him a millionaire by the time he was twenty-one.

Sure, he got an allowance, a weekly allowance of $2.50! Not much so far as riches go, but he still managed to buy presents for his mother and his baby sister Renee. His companion/tutor, Mrs. Ardena Johnston, said at the time: "Sometimes he spends it all, and then he whispers in my ear, 'I'm broke.' I whisper back, 'I'm broke, too.' We hope to teach him to use his money wisely, to avoid champagne tastes."

They succeeded, as we'll see later: He never developed a taste for champagne. Expensive recording equipment, now, that's another set of tunes.

Little Stevie Wonder was on his way to becoming a star. It would be nice to report that everyone around rejoiced in his good fortune. But, indeed, no. There was jealousy and envy around. He was repeatedly mobbed at school, until his mother took him out of it and enrolled him at the Michigan School for the Blind in Lansing (approximately 150 miles from Detroit).

On the road—his traveling increased the older he grew—he studied with a tutor.

At Lansing, he was taught to read Braille

music. He took violin, piano, and string bass lessons. He loved the bass and played it in the school orchestra. He also participated with enthusiasm in the physical education program: he swam, he wrestled, he skated, and he even went bowling.

Of school subjects, he liked history best, closely followed by science. By history, he meant world history. He found the history of this country relatively boring. But to hear about civilizations, old civilizations existing long before ours and what happened to them, was something he liked. (He has kept a sense of history. In his song, "Big Brother," he speaks of history, the heritage of violence . . . the inherited negative blindness of not being able to see what's going on, particularly with minority people.)

He saw little of his family at this time. He missed them and felt lonely sometimes. Often he talked to his mother on the phone and felt her constant support even when she wasn't there physically.

But his life was structured. Meals and bedtimes were regularly kept up. He was taught the principles of hard work and honesty.

And success began to appear as a frequent guest in his life. Soon it was going to be a live-in companion.

In 1963, he made "Fingertips," that wildcat hit that remained on the singles charts for fifteen weeks. Stevie sang, played harmonica (backed by a big band). The record climbed to number one on record charts throughout the country. One critic wrote, "His raw, joyous harmonica jumps out like sparks from a welding torch."

Then his first LP, *12 Year Old Genius* (though he was 13 at the time), was released, and Stevie became nationally famous. He was talked about as being a phenomenon. He has never ceased to be one.

The very first thing he recorded, by the way, was something called "Mother Thank You," which title pleased him. Originally it had been called "You Made a Wow," but that was decided to be too "lovey" for him, too adult.

He also had a chance to pay a debt from early listening days by recording the hit album, *A Tribute to Uncle Ray*, all vocals. It was, of course, the fabulous Ray Charles whom he saluted.

The wonderful world of Little Stevie Wonder, blind teenage musician on his way to super-stardom, was brand new and shiny.

The excitement of applause, traveling, and meeting entertainment greats enthralled the young Detroiter. All around him was the glittery, tinseled, brightly illuminated world of show business. His sightless eyes could not see it, he could only hear and feel it. Maybe that's why it didn't distract him in damaging ways. Instead he developed the *secret* world of Steve Wonder, the world where he played the music he loved, and his keenly attuned ears heard distant sounds, where he experimented. His own voice taught him the nearly limitless possibilities of the human voice.

On a big stage, slender and small before the great piano, he seemed remote, in another world. His head moved constantly as if keeping time to some ethereal beat, coming from outer space.

He was always learning, wherever he was.

He learned from some of the finest musicians in the country, he learned in recording studios and on stage. He toured and learned more. When he was sixteen, he had played throughout Europe and America, always eager to find out things beyond the stage and the dressing rooms. He wanted to know about customs of the places, how people lived, thought, what they felt, what made them laugh or cry.

Sometimes, his enthusiasm got the better of him. It happened that he did not want to leave the stage when it was time to do so. A few times he had to be picked up and carried off!

Once, during a concert, he upstaged fellow Motown singer Marvin Gaye. Afterwards he went around to apologize. "I didn't want to burn you, Marv. You're the greatest. I just wanted to make people happy."

"Sure," said Gaye, "and I'm putting arsenic in your tea for lunch."

"The hits kept comin'," as they say. Why didn't all the success spoil him? Why didn't he become an unbearable brat?

For one thing, he remained close to his

family. He kept going back to his Detroit neighborhood, sought out old friends, spent time with them.

"I grew up in the streets with my friends in spite of all that," he said once, thinking back to those early years. "And a lot of people at Motown took good care of me. It was a very beautiful love and warmth."

He spent years on tour with the Motown Revue. Went from hotel to hotel, traveled from city to city, always finding bright lights warming his face, big stages to be filled with music, and hordes of strangers who turned into cheering admirers.

Other performers would joke about not wanting to sleep in the hotel room next to his because he'd keep them awake bumping into the walls, they said. That used to break Stevie up, because he rarely bumped into anything. His hearing had become so keen that he could recognize the slightest accoustical change as he approached something solid, like a wall.

"Sound happens all the time, *all* the time," he points out. "Sound bounces off everything, there's always something happening."

Through his ears and his other senses, Stevie saw everything. "When you're traveling on the road, you have to learn to get to know yourself, always know where you are as a person, what your likes are. I had to learn this at a very young age, and fast."

Oh yes, he needed to know who he was and what he wanted, because everything did not just fall over him effortlessly. There came a period when he was about seventeen, when things calmed down a bit. He was no longer the fantastic boy genius and he was not yet a man. His voice, too, had changed, and he had to adjust to that.

At the same time, he became more aware of some of the less pretty things in the world around him. One month before he turned 18, Martin Luther King was assassinated. Stevie had met Dr. King twice and calls him "a man who will always have a place in my heart." The second time Dr. King met him, the older man told the young man that he was very proud of what Stevie had already done for his people.

My people? He began to realize – maybe it took longer because he was blind and had learned to live in an inner, secret world where the color scheme was different – that he was a black man. A poor black man originally.

In Detroit there were race riots.

There were three, four years of adjustment for Stevie the artist as well as for Stevie the human being.

He thought back. He remembered things. He remembered how they sometimes had to steal coal in Saginaw so they could heat the home. He remembered remarks, attitudes, what he had overheard and sensed. He also thought of how he wanted the world to be. He acknowledged what was and decided to work to bring about changes.

He kept living with music. He listened to the Beatles. He liked the echoes, the voice effects, the writing. It revealed to him that he could be freer, looser, that he could reach for other places and needn't stay in one key all the time.

He didn't like those who preached negativism, hate, hopelessness, those who didn't believe in the possibility of change. To this day, he protests loudly when people find out that he was born on May 13th and that his sun sign therefore is Taurus, the bull, and come up with statements to the effect that Taureans don't like change too much. "I say as long as it's change to widen your horizons, it's cool," he comments.

He listened to Bob Dylan and recorded Dylan's "Blowin' in the Wind" during the '60s (a few years ago, Wonder and Dylan appeared together at a benefit concert at the Houston Astrodome).

He listened to Brazilian music.

The mid-'60s offered him a variety of styles ... There were Jimi Hendrix, the Beach Boys, the Grateful Dead ...

Black artists began to come into their own as never before: James Brown, Aretha Franklin, the Supremes, the Temptations and many more.

Their music was loaded to the brim with emotion, earlier blues were defined, gospel and jazz were mixed in – the music became known as *soul music*.

45

Soul music influenced everyone on the music scene. It set new standards for all music.

In 1965, Stevie's *Up-tight* had been released and had a tremendous impact. There was the excitement of soul! He had written *Up-tight* himself. More and more, he began to record his own material. His sound became more original, more highly personal.

"I Was Made To Love Her" was another incredible hit (1967). It offered a strong beat but kept the melody well and alive.

By the time he was seventeen, Stevie had come out with nine albums and eighteen singles — and LITTLE was dropped from his name.

Toward the end of the '60s, he began to break away from the "Motown sound" of the time. "My Cherie Amour" in 1969 is a good example. As is "For Once In My Life," a rearrangement of a Broadway musical song. These two are more haunting ballads than soul tunes. The funky, grinding backgrounds of his early records were replaced by a sophisticated, silky stream of swelling strings and brass.

Was he moving away from soul?

"I like pretty songs, melodies that stick with you," he said simply. "Pretty tunes are coming back, tunes that are melodic but not too melodic, tunes with melodies you can't get away from."

And about soul: "I don't think soul belongs to any one race or group of people. It belongs to anyone who's able to arouse strong emotions. The Beatles, John and Paul, Frank Sinatra, Ray Charles—they all got soul. A lot of black people have just started digging the Beatles and a lot of white people have just started digging B.B. King. That's the kind of things that'll get people together."

The romantic "fluff" he had written in his early teenage years interested him less. The romantic, bubbly, extremely popular songs to dance to no longer suited him.

Where I'm Coming From was the title of the last album Stevie made under his old arrangement with Motown. It may have been his not so subtle way of telling the executives there what he meant and what he wanted.

Increased awareness as a person and as an artist, but how about Stevie at this time as a young man? He was searching in that area too and with great enthusiasm—there was a long line of girlfriends.

One young lady will not forget him—others echo the same sentiment.

"He was around nineteen or twenty. First I thought it would be kind of, you know . . . *uncomfortable* . . . to go out with a blind guy. I mean, he was cute and all that, really nice smile and tall and slim. But blind—what do you do? Cut the meat on his plate? But I didn't feel that I was the greatest thing since mashed potatoes so I cheered myself up by thinking, 'At least he can't see that my nose isn't perfect.' Sure, it was a little weird but it was *nice* weird. I mean, it didn't take me long to forget that he was blind. He moves around so easily, he doesn't fumble or stumble. And he talks as if he could see. D'you know what he told me? He told me that I had very warm eyes!

'How would you know that?' I said. I can feel them shining in me,' he said. Imagine that! *I can feel them shining in me.*

"I felt beautiful with him. I think he can . . . sense who people are. If they're silly or phony.

"It was terrific. Not because he's a star . . . well, that, too . . . but he's a super person, too.

"It must be difficult to be in love with him, I mean really in love and living with him. He's . . . he's different. I'd imagine if there were some beautiful race on another planet . . . like some stories tell it . . . people who are wiser and better than we are . . . I could imagine Stevie actually having been put down here from some planet like that . . .

"He does live in another world. The things he thinks of . . . and he talks about loving others and he means it. If someone else did that, it would be silly. You'd feel like saying, 'Hey, man, take that Norman Vincent Peale act somewhere else – why don't you become a preacher? 'People don't talk about holding out hands to others . . . about understanding . . . about hate and envy eating up your insides . . . about children being like flowers . . . It isn't tough or with it . . . The world is harsh and you're not in Sunday school any-

Even with his busy schedule of composing, touring and recording, Stevie always has time to spend with his lovely wife, Yolanda, and his daughter, Aisha Zakia, whose birth inspired the infectious and popular song, "Isn't She Lovely?"

Stevie Wonder is a complex man given to periods of silent contemplation. He is sensitive, not only to his music, but to the world around him. The environment, human kindness and the search for world peace are high on his list of causes which are constantly reflected in his work.

51

At the celebration of Martin Luther King's birthday in Atlanta, Georgia, Wonder shares a thought with then U.N. Ambassador Andrew Young.

Music has always been the center of Stevie Wonder's universe. As a young child the radio was his best friend. He learned to hear each instrument separately in his mind, and he soon decided that if they could do it, so could he. Wonder is seen here recording what was to become his biggest selling album, Songs in the Key of Life.

Stevie Wonder is so versatile that he can easily perform with anyone. Just back from a tour with the Rolling Stones, he and Sammy Davis, Jr. mix their vocal talents to the delight of their fans.

Upon graduation from the Michigan School for the Blind, Wonder receives a plaque for an "awe-inspiring life, which he has so brilliantly and outstandingly lived each and every day," presented by Michigan State Representative George Edwards.

George Benson and Peter Frampton share the stage with Stevie Wonder at the 1977 Grammy Awards. Wonder's album, Songs in the Key of Life, *walked away with most of the top honors.*

Bob Marley and the Wailers, Jamaica's top reggae group, get a little help from Stevie Wonder on "Stand Up For Your Rights," a reggae tune that drove a Philadelphia crowd to feverish heights.

Smokey Robinson and Stevie at gala celebration of Wonder's birthday. The party was held at the Speak-easy in Hollywood and was attended by some of the biggest stars in the industry.

Stevie doing what he does best. He loves people, and the bigger the audience the better the performance. Wonder's music brings a message of peace and harmony to the world.

Elton John and Barry White share the stage with Stevie Wonder at yet another presentation. Wonder has won more Grammys than any other recording artist.

Stevie's mother, one of the biggest influences in his life, starts the birthday celebration at the Speakeasy by cutting the birthday cake. His mother has always encouraged him to rely on himself. She was always the first to say, "you can do it." And he's certainly proved that he could!

Wonder's first marriage to lovely Syreeta Wright ended in divorce. However they remained close, and she still writes some of his lyrics. Her latest work was the vocals on "Come Back as a Flower," from the album, The Secret Life of Plants.

Wonder makes magical music with every instrument he plays, but his best instrument has always been his voice. He began writing songs at the age of ten and recorded his first one when he was only twelve, hence the nickname, "Little Stevie Wonder." The "Little" stuck with him for years.

63

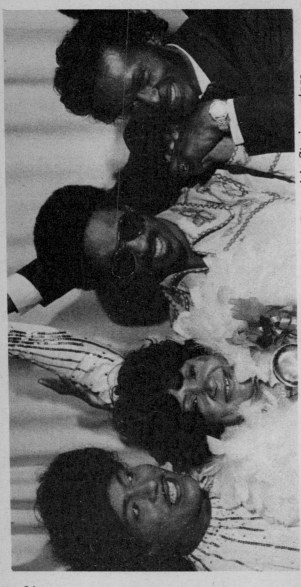

Little Richard, Stevie's mother and the great Chuck Berry join Stevie on stage as he was presented with yet another award.

more. But with Stevie . . . well it's *real*. And he's right, you know. I think it takes a special kind of guts to be like he is . . . and I think we need more people like that. I know that he's touched me . . . I'm not exactly as I'd be if I'd never known him. It's as if . . . as if he taught me to *see* more . . ."

CHAPTER THREE

Do you ever wake up in the morning with a feeling that the day is like a coiled spring, waiting for you to give it some purpose? That you're looking for some hidden key, some secret password that'll tell you how to live, what to do, what decisions to make, what values to honor?

We all come to crossroads now and then. Sometimes one road is known and "safe" while the other one means risks, challenges, facing the unknown, maybe being criticized, not being popular.

Every artist faces choices—and since all people have creativity in them, all face choices.

At the beginning of the '70s Stevie Wonder had left the teens behind. What now?

Why change? Why not hold onto a good thing? His records were selling, the Motown sound was defined and increasingly popular—why rock the boat?

By now, he had decided that he knew enough to produce his own records. He wanted to have control over all aspects of his recordings: musicians, arrangers, and engineers. He wanted total artistic freedom.

During his twentieth year he faced many a morning filled with choices, spent many a restless night pondering what he wanted to do, really wanted.

Frequently, he exhausted the people around him. What was he fretting about? Hadn't he come a long, long way from Detroit's ghetto? What more did he want? He had fame, he had girls. And it wasn't as if he needed the money either.

1971 rolled around. An earthquake shook Los Angeles, and Stevie celebrated his twenty-first birthday. Among other things, that meant that he took control of the money which had accumulated for him in trust over the years. He was a millionaire! He had sold an estimated 35 million records—and now he made the decision: He was going to become a real musical artist! On *his* terms!

Stevie Wonder left Motown in 1971. "I want to go somewhere else," he said.

He felt that the pressure to produce hit after hit hampered his search for new sounds, his lust to experiment, to grow and develop.

He left Detroit and family and headed for the city of New York.

He wandered the streets, heard the hum of the city, smelled its ripeness, was pushed and shoved, heard the street talk, the money talk, the lonely talk. He was looking for his hidden keys, his secret passwords.

He spent hours upon hours in recording studios, putting the music that filled his inner self onto tapes.

He paid for everything with his own money.

Nobody else told him what to do, how to do it, when to do it. He set his own rules. He recorded exactly what he felt. In one ten day period, he completed about forty tunes.

In between, he talked to people. All kinds of people. Experts and junkies. He went to offices of record companies, looking for the one that would give him the kind of freedom he craved.

He found such a record company. Its name was – Motown!

Motown offered him a new deal, one that satisfied him totally.

With his lawyer, Johanan Vigoda, Stevie negotiated an unprecedented contract. Motown would distribute his records. Stevie would have total artistic control, his own production company, and a percentage of the royalties that is reported to have been fifty percent.

He had had two earlier contracts with Motown. For this, his third contract, negotiations went on for six weeks and the contract itself was 120 pages long.

He never discussed the details. All he said was that he felt "secure."

The contract was important to Stevie, but it was also important to Motown. In the words of Vgota (who also negotiated contracts for Jimi Hendrix, Richie Havens, and others): "Stevie broke tradition with the deal, legally, professionally – in terms of how he could cut his records and where he could cut – and in breaking tradition he opened up the future for Motown. They had never had an *artist* in 13 years, they had single records, they managed to create a name in certain areas, but they never came through with a major, major artist. It turned out they did a beautiful job."

"It was time for a change musically," Stevie says. "Spiritually I had gone as far as I could have gone."

Stevie's whole environment had been transformed. He had definitely moved out of his family's home and was living in a New York City hotel for a while. And he got married.

"I then asked the questions again of where

am I going, what am I going to do? I had to see and feel what I wanted to do and feel what my destiny was; the direction of destiny anyway, and we got into *Music of My Mind*. I think that when you gradually change you still have a certain thing that you left behind. When you take a very abrupt change, you say 'okay boom' this is what this is going to be about – click and you do that. It's like you can't gradually leave a kind of music. You have to do whatever you feel you want to do musically. You can't mix a concept with another kind."

The resulting album was an even more radical departure from the familiar Motown sound than anyone expected. It was recorded independently at the Electric Lady studios in New York with Stevie playing all the instruments (with some work added by his band) and with strong emphasis on the Moog and Arp synthesizers.

"The synthesizer has allowed me to do a lot of things I've wanted to do for a long time, but which were not possible until it came along. It has added a whole new dimension to music," he said. He talked lovingly about the Moog as "a way to directly express what comes from your mind" – hence, the title of the album.

Music of My Mind was Stevie's work, not Motown's. Therefore, it was not calculated, as had all of Stevie's previous work been, for Top 40 popularity. Instead it was designed to open up his music as far as it would go, to break out of the style established for him over the years.

"I'm not trying to be different. I'm just trying to be myself," he tried to explain.

Stevie did all the vocals, composed all the music, wrote most of the lyrics (though he co-wrote with Syreeta, his wife of one year), and produced the album.

It was so fresh, so new, that even Stevie began to worry. How would people react? Could they take "Superwoman?" "Little Girl Blue?" Would the listeners feel for the multi-textured electronic sounds as he did or anywhere near that? If he could not transmit his feelings to others, then he had failed. Failed to communicate. To him music was—and is—communication between human beings.

"Music is like a religion to me," he said. "The more sharing that takes place between the musicians and the audience, the more spiritual the music becomes."

People had to understand what he was saying. Understanding comes first. Without it, there can be no sharing.

People bought his record, listened, grew fascinated. Enough seemed to understand.

Enough? Did he reach enough people?

Who were his audiences?

They were predominantly black.

Stevie decided that he wanted to cross over, wanted to raise society's consciousness about black people. He wanted to reach over and across racial barriers. He realized that black music still reached mainly black audiences while "white music" (even if less than authentic) reached *all* audiences. What he had to say concerned anybody who wanted to be concerned. It was about life. About struggle, yes. About protests, yes. He believed he had something to say, something important, that ought to be said to *all* people. It's one world or should be – let's try to understand each other, he seemed to plead. He realized the stupidity that closed many minds, but still he believed there were enough people out there who would grasp his message about life, truth, and love.

That's why he chose to associate himself with the Rolling Stones temporarily.

In June of 1972, the Rolling Stones, the English group proclaiming themselves to be "the greatest rock and roll band in the world," toured America for the first time in over two years. The tour was described by many as "sensational!"

Stevie Wonder became part of it. He opened the show from Vancouver to New York – fifty days, fifty concerts. Ironically, the last time he had played with the Rolling Stones was back in 1964 – when Stevie had top billing.

Is there an irony in this? Didn't the Stones get what they know, their beat, from rhythm and blues, from gospel, from Chuck Berry and company? Don't they owe a tremendous debt – don't all white rock musicians – to black music? One could speculate where popular music would be today if one somehow went back and erased black music and its far-reaching, enormous influence on the whole music scene. Or, as somebody said, "The blacks made the music—the whites made the money."

Stevie didn't speculate about who owed what to whom. He knew what he was doing. It all was connected with his recent musical changes and a conscious plan to expand his audiences.

"I felt it was the kind of people that we should get to, so I thought we should do it."

The fans of the Stones went wild over the new Wonder.

"It was like his voice was nothing but emotion, melted emotion, that flowed from him to the crowd, without interruptions. It surrounded all of us. We were together, united somehow, in a special sound, a very, very special feeling."

1973. Stevie worked at break-neck speed. Eight hours, ten hours, fourteen hours in the studio almost without a break. Night and day floated into each other—to Stevie it made no difference. To those around him it was hard sometimes. He exhausted his staff.

He was driven. Restless energy drove him on and on. Did he take mega-vitamins or did he chew on sticks of dynamite? Sometimes, it was as if he wanted to go out and paint his messages in big angry letters on the walls of houses, on fences, shout his words from roof tops, holler it to all around, shake them up, wake them.

Bursting with frantic energy that never let up, he kept on. It was as if he did his work with "God looking over his shoulder." This was the time when he was haunted by the feeling that something was going to happen. He had to say what he wanted, had to open some eyes.

Then BOOM! – it happened. The car accident. With the force that's peculiar to nature, he was put on his back and kept still. Whatever happened inside Stevie Wonder during those days in a coma and the forced inactivity some weeks afterwards, he came out of it filled with exuberance and the splendor and magnificence of life to a greater degree than before.

To say that Stevie Wonder before the accident was totally different than Stevie Wonder after the accident would be not to understand the constant growth of this man. Any concern evidenced afterwards can be seen in his earlier works as well. It may be safe to say that the jolt of the accident, in combination with his ongoing growth, brought out a keener-than-ever awareness, a more personal than ever voice.

Being intent on having something to say, being quite serious about getting a message through to us, Stevie never forgets that his main function is that of a musician. Right when the message becomes the thing, he'll stop and break in with some beautiful vocal and/or instrumental touch.

"I'm an entertainer, not a politician, not a preacher," he'll say. "Of course, should I happen to enlighten someone about something, that's only good." And he'll grin. He knows what he's doing! Yeah, the man is his music!

Now and then, he "makes history." Being honored as few have in the Grammy Awards of both 1974 and 1975, there arrived the day – August 5, 1975 – when he did it again: The biggest contract in the history of the record industry was concluded between Stevie Wonder and Motown Record Corporation.

The agreement called for guarantees to Stevie over a seven year period of more than 13 million dollars. (This sum was equal to the deals of Elton John and Neil Diamond *combined*, it was pointed out at the time.)

Headlines proclaimed the unprecedented contract and words like "authentic genius" were used by other recording artists, producers, and the general public. Stevie remained his cool, philosophical self.

"Of course I'm happy about it, but there is something perhaps even more important involved," he said in a press release.

"I'm staying at Motown because it is the only viable surviving black-owned company in the record industry.

"Motown represents hope and opportunity for new as well as established black performers and producers. If it were not for Motown, many of us just wouldn't have had the shot we've had at success and fulfillment.

"In the record industry we've all seen many cases where the big companies eat up the little ones and I didn't want this to happen to Motown. I feel young black children should have something to look up to.

"It is vital that the people in our business—particularly the black creative community including artists, writers, and producers—make sure that Motown stays emotionally stable, spiritually strong, and economically healthy."

Ewart Abner, president of the Motown Records division of Motown Industries, spearheaded the negotiations for the landmark pact.

"It is difficult to translate Stevie's special kind of creative genius as an artist, producer and writer to a dollar sign," Abner said.

"When a performer gets to the plateau that Stevie owns, he stands alone and it is obvious he could command just about anything he wanted with any record company in the world.

"That is why we at Motown are especially gratified with Stevie's philosophy that he can best help his brothers and sisters by keeping Motown strong so there will be a marketplace for their creative talents."

Abner emphasized Stevie Wonder being in a class by himself. "Stevie is the only artist ever to win ten Grammys over a two-year period, winning five in 1974 and five again in 1975."

Yes, indeed, in a class by himself. In his last two albums he had played all of the instruments himself. His latest six albums had all been *gold (Fulfillingness' First Finale, Innervisions, Talking Book, Music of My Mind, Stevie Wonder's Greatest Hits Vol.2,* and *Stevie Wonder's Greatest Hits).*

That same year, he was nominated for more awards than any other performer or producer for the First Annual Rock Awards, presented in a TV-special co-hosted by Diana Ross and Elton John.

Also in 1975, he was the recipient of the National Association of Record Merchandisers' Presidential Award. He was the youngest and first black honoree for this award given by an organization representing about eighty percent of all record buyers in the United States.

By now, Stevie had started the trend of the do-it-all artists: writing, producing, arranging, playing all the instruments, doing all the vocals. This had been considered virtually impossible until he came along. Equally amazing is that he did all this remaining true to himself, remaining accessible to listeners (nobody needs a degree in music theory to understand Stevie), and without being cutely commercial.

His importance when it comes to influencing other artists is, naturally, tremendous. Of the most recent ones, Prince, eleven years younger than Stevie, comes to mind as already showing signs of being one of those originals that doesn't fit into a mold. Stevie paved the way.

An artist such as Stevie is extremely rare. He represents values that go far beyond material concerns. Then he tops it off by being honestly modest. He may even wrinkle his nose at the word *artist*. He senses the creativity all people have in them, dormant or not, he respects that and speaks to it and doesn't want to set himself miles apart due to some inborn ability or talent.

He knows that it's not how many records he has sold, how many polls he has won, how many top charts he has made that define his value. He puts the importance on the person, on being a good person, a real human being.

This human being-ness combined with talent keeps him fresh. He wants to create always something that's never been before just because he feels it strongly inside.

These attitudes led to *Songs in the Key of Life,* the album he worked on for two years. It took it just one week to reach the top of the pop charts (the first double LP – 21 cuts – to get there so quickly).

It is rich as life – jazz and samba and soul and pop. It celebrates the total human experience, it declares the absolute need for greater understanding among people. Survival through love, is the message.

"Stevie stands alone." "The album is a tour de force." "Wonder's masterpiece." Reviewers kept finding more and more adjectives to apply to the sense of Wonder they experienced.

He himself said that he simply wanted to touch on some of the most important experiences in life to show how very much we all have in common.

Again, an artist has two main roads to choose from. Maybe the rest of us have these same two choices. Either you do what you have done that worked before. Keep dong it. Play it safe. Keep giving your audiences (or your boss, your family, your friends) what they have come to expect, what they think they want. Or else you keep experimenting, growing, startling, doing what nobody expected, eager to live and work and please not others but yourself. That means taking risks.

It's clear to which category Stevie belongs. He said in an interview, "It's all about pleasing myself. Not everybody and anybody but pleasing myself. I'm the hardest person for me to please."

And also, "I do the best I can, no matter how long it takes."

That's the only guarantee Stevie gives us, that he'll keep giving us his best, whatever it is at that moment in time. Whatever visions, dreams, insights, sudden thoughts, bits of knowledge, experiences, inspirations, emotions, moments, expressions he comes up with, he'll share them with us.

Life is a labyrinth, he seems to have found. Each one of us may interpret it differently.

Most of humanity may be content to crawl around the outer edges of this labyrinth, perhaps occasionally venturing a short distance into it before withdrawing in fear. But Stevie sets out for the heart of the labyrinth, telling us about every bit of the winding way, recording changes, handing us pieces of pulsating life.

He has dropped a lot of the rules concerning "good" and "bad." He obeyes only his own instincts and intuitions. He has stopped bothering with the "ifs" and "buts" and just *does*.

"If nobody paid Stevie," says one of his friends "he'd be entertaining on the nearest street corner."

"You know why we all need guys like Stevie?" asks a musician. "He means better health in the business. There's constant pressure in this business to repeat your last success. It's weird and it's corrupt and few have the strength to rebel against it. Stevie does and we all benefit from it. So do you!"

CHAPTER FOUR

The trouble with writing Stevie Wonder's life story is that it doesn't follow the rules. We know the formula from other biographies of entertainers, from movies and books. First, there should be obscurity and poverty (sure, but only until the age of ten), struggle (he went from success to success), fame (oh yes), pain and confusion (there must have been—we find hints in his songs—but he's such an *optimist*), drugs (not at all), and resolution (he just keeps growing). How do you write *believably* about someone who was discovered as a child, keeps doing well, believes in love and honesty and discipline, remains a perfectionist, leads a clean life, and even loves his mother? The money has rolled in, and some has rolled out—but to charities and recording equipment, not to fanciful living. This is not a pain-filled life with an occasional peak—he seems to live his life on mountain tops. His life is a major chord of joy!

Love is his theme and quite often he sings about personal, romantic love.

He jokes about how he was a "real menace" to the opposite sex before he got married but is also careful to point out that at no time did he "mess with no married woman. No way, never. I would not."

He knows that his fame was part of his attraction. The probelm with fame is not knowing if another person is attracted to the public image, the fame, or to the person.

"I used to meet girls and I'd say, 'You know me as Stevie Wonder but I want you to know me like I am. I mean, eventually I'm going to stop singing.' And she'd say, 'No, no, you can't stop singing.' And I'd say, 'But my name is really Steve Judkins.' And she'd say, 'Yeah, but you'll always be Little Stevie Wonder to me, baby!!'"

Then when he was 21, he married Syreeta Wright, a singer-songwriter and sometime transcendental meditation teacher, who worked at Motown as a secretary. Wonder's arranger suggested that he write her a song.

"I heard her sing and she sounded good so I said okay," Stevie remembers. The song never came out, but when the two met in the studio, it was "very good vibes."

The marriage lasted eighteen months. What happened? He talks about the break-up in some songs, but privately he prefers not to discuss it. He has not been heard to say anything but good things about Syreeta. "She's a beautiful person," he'll say. Though once he commented that to put a Leo (Syreeta is a Leo) with a Taurus (which is what Stevie is) is like putting two sticks of dynamite together.

Syreeta will say, "Stevie taught me that a person's biggest influence should be his own heart."

A certain closeness has remained. Some are surprised that two divorced people have been able to remain friends, but evidently these two have. On his latest album, *The Secret Life of Plants*, Syreeta wrote the lyrics and did some of the vocals for the song "Come Back As a Flower."

One could speculate about the reasons for the divorce. Was it Syreeta's strong wish for a career? Does Stevie need a woman who lives completely for him? Were there too many people around Stevie? Too many hangers-on? Did she only get small pieces of him? Some people have suggested that Stevie has a bit of the male chauvinist in him, and they quote lyrics from "Superwoman" to prove a point. That may be. It may also be that being blind – and never using a cane or a guide dog – Stevie remains dependent on someone for many of life's everyday things.

The same year Stevie and Syreeta broke up (1973), he met Yolanda Simmons, whom he calls "Londie." They first met on the phone when she was looking for a job as secretary/bookkeeper at his publishing company, Black Bull. Stevie liked the way she sounded, and they became friends. The friendship developed into love.

Yolanda, a tall, graceful, sensitive woman, one year younger than Stevie, seems to have understood Stevie and his needs from the first. She also seems to have realized what few do: that love and possession are not the same thing. Set that free which you love and it'll return to you. A man such as Stevie who lives with and for his music to such an unusual extent would have problems with a woman who demanded a man around the house most of the time. Yolanda is there when he needs her, but she is also independent. When Stevie is somewhere else, be it days or weeks at a time, she fills her life (among other things with transcendental meditation and fashion design).

Since 1975, she has had her hands full with their child.

That was a fine year for Stevie Wonder. Early in that year, he settled his pregnant Yolanda in a brownstone house on East 18th

Street in New York City. Then in March he received five Grammys (one of these he accepted in memory of Elijah Muhammad and Jack Benny—some combination).

But on April 7, 1975, he received the "biggest Grammy" of them all. The newspaper announcement read as follows:

*"A girl Aisha Zakia 8 lbs
April 7 at St. Luke's Hospital, New York
to Stevie Wonder and Yolanda."*

The name Aisha Zakia is African and means *life* and *intelligence*.

The song about her, "Isn't She Lovely?" grabs the heart of just about any listener. There the essence of Stevie's art is distilled in the most perfect way. The song is punctuated by live nursery sound effects. It gives the impression that it was created, sung, and recorded with one thing only in mind: to grab hold of one exalted, fantastic moment of happiness and translate it into a song.

Such statements of love and birth accompanied by irresistible rhythm will keep on revitalizing pop music in general. His sheer force as a musician, his intelligence, his vitality and energy could sometimes make other pop albums sound, well, a little bit on the drowsy side.

Stevie remains a happy, proud father and sometimes threatens to have a couple of dozen more kids. "Aisha is just like me," he'll say. "She's into everything. She's full of surprises."

He is full of surprises and likes to do dramatic things.

As when he came out with *Songs in the Key of Life* after two years without releasing an album. (When Paul Simon in 1976 accepted the Grammy for best album, he thanked Stevie Wonder for not making an album during 1975.) To celebrate the release, Stevie invited 76 members of the press to a farm in New England to hear the record before it was issued.

He made a dramatic entrance dressed in an eggwhite-colored Tom Mix cowboy outfit with a gun belt that said "Number One with a Bullet" on the back and two of his albums hanging as holsters!

It was slightly bizarre: a black, blind, urban artist presenting his new record at a farm in Massachusetts, dressed like a musical comedy version of a Western sheriff.

(That farm, by the way, is rented only to rock groups—for around 1,500 dollars a day. The price is high but it includes a rustic ranch house that sleeps twenty, complete and good recording facilities, a stable of thoroughbreds—oh yes, Stevie loves horseback riding—and the special "yeast bombs," high energy protein-vitamin drinks that are said to pep up the most played-out of musicians.)

He is a mixture of the dramatic and the simple. He stood there in his Western costume and said simply, "I hope you enjoy this.

But it really doesn't matter. I gave it my all and all is the best I can do."

For another album preview, he blindfolded the music press in the studio, took them for a bus ride, and kept them in the dark through dinner so they could "hear what Stevie hears."

In spite of his flair for the dramatic, Stevie remains square by rock standards. He does not drink, and he has smoked pot only twice and "it scared me to death."

That's right. He doesn't drink at all since the accident and never much before it, though then he took a little beer now and then and "sometimes a little Mateus." But he cut out the wine when he heard what the Portuguese were doing in Angola. He never did acid or any hard drugs. About his two experiences with pot, he says that the first time he tried grass "it was pretty nice," but the next time it was nothing but "a lot of paranoia so I never went near it again."

This often comes as a surprise to people. Many have trouble believing it, even. They feel he must be using *something* to feel as good as he seems to do much of the time. It is difficult to realize that one *can* get high on life itself.

Audiences make him high. (He seems chemically free of stage fright.) The clarinet makes him high. The electric piano wired to an ARP-2100 synthesizer producing that insistent sound that gets to you, penetrates deep inside your brain, gives him a tremendous high. As does the mixing of madrigals and rock blasts.

If he is addicted to anything, he is addicted to the telephone. He keeps up long conversations at odd hours, and sometimes he carries on two conversations at once, switching back and forth. He is a fantastic voice mimic, and loves it if he's able to fool his friends. By now, most of them know that if they hear a crazy voice saying way-out things in English or Spanish or some African dialect, chances are it's just little ol' Stevie.

Among his favorite impersonations: a Southern redneck . . . a white hustler . . . also a black one . . . a frantic disc jockey . . . an English lord . . . a little Jewish city kid.

His voice is his main instrument, a flexible tool. He uses it when he gets angry, too. He has said several times that he has trouble understanding a man who beats a woman. He finds other ways than violence to release his own anger. To beat up someone is vulgar to him. In a rage, his voice is his best weapon. (There is one thing that could make him dangerously violent, he admits: if someone messed with his child.)

But he says that he used to be jealous in love matters. "Yeah, I used to worry about when I went with someone that they'd be doing something with somebody else. I didn't show my jealousy but I was. But . . . when you realize that nothing really belongs to you, you begin to appreciate having an understanding of just where your head is at, and you feel so much better."

"Stevie has 20/20 vision in his ears," a friend says. And Ira Tucker can tell about the time in Puerto Rico when the sun was shining with all its might and Stevie kept insisting it was going to rain. He said he could feel the moisture in the air. Everybody laughed. Three hours later, sure enough, down it came. A hailstorm!

He even turns the light on and off when he goes to the bathroom. Why? Because everybody else does it, he says. "*Click*, you go in, *click*, you're out."

The only real signs of his blindness are his black glasses and his habit of moving his head back and forth, side to side, when he feels good. He calls that a "blindism" and explains that sighted people use up a lot of energy just by the act of seeing. A sightless person has all that extra energy stored up and often develops some little habit to use it up.

"Sometimes I wish I could drive a car," he says and adds, "But I'm gonna drive a car one day so I don't worry about that."

Drive a car?! "I've flown a plane before. A Cessna or something. From Chicago to New York. Scared the hell out of everybody. Of course, the regular pilot was there all the time."

In his songs, he uses colors to describe things. He insists that he has a good idea what colors are, that he associates them with what he has been told about certain colors. "I get a feeling in my head when a person says red or blue or green or black or white . . . purple is a crazy color to me."

He actually *sees* music. "Each instrument has its own color. The piano for instance is dark brown. It's like a puzzle and when I fit all the pieces together, that's my high."

He loves to explore new places, new smells, new sounds, new feelings in the air, new and specific "vibrations" for want of a better word.

He loves to talk. He has a way of getting to people, getting anyone to really open up. Sometimes he'll begin by talking about astrological signs. Sometimes he talks like a tough street kid, breaks the grammar into little hard pieces, peppers his language with slang. Other times he sounds like a preacher or a prophet. There are times when he sounds too good to be true, too sweet, too optimistic. But what would be platitudes in someone else's mouth become believable in his. Happy thoughts like curlicues delivered with that enormous grin turn into pearls of wisdom. "Yeah, that's it!" one wants to say.

There are times when he talks about the destruction of the earth, of oceans, of our lack of respect for other living things on our planet, of our destruction of ourselves. Sometimes he'll talk about his own death and what he hopes to leave behind for those still left.

"Sometimes I feel like an old person, seeing all the changes in me and in the business. The music business moves fast. All those that have died. Suddenly. Needlessly sometimes. But that may be their karma."

Whatever he talks about, he comes back to music. Everything is related to music. He lives with his music many hours a day. Everything is in it: an Afro consciousness, jazz, soul, rock, synthesized music, old hits, bits of other people's songs. He moves from drums to electric piano to ARP-wired clavinet to guitar to harmonica – a one-man band with energy for ten.

How does he write a song? Where does he get his ideas?

"Oh, I listen to a lot of people. I hear a phrase, a certain riff. That's how we all come up with ideas. It's the same thing as reading somebody's poem or learning somebody else's steps. Some ideas are blown into your head by the wind. Maybe angels whisper in your ear when you're asleep."

The melody usually comes first, he says. Then, later, he writes the lyrics. Most of the time he comes up with one line and works around it.

"Certain weeks you can write and then the next week you can't. But you can't be getting worried when it doesn't come."

One thing though he finds horrible: When he dreams wonderful, magic music, but forgets it the moment he awakens. He shudders when he thinks of great tunes that may have gotten away.

Is it the music that makes him able to sense phony people, that makes him cut through a lot of bull?

Does he see people and their characteristics *musically*? It sounds strange, but the other year he was interviewed on TV by Barbara Walters. He was himself—shy, softspoken, quietly intense. The highlight of the interview was when he sat down at the piano and composed melodies he thought reflected his own and Walters' personalities!

Honors keep raining on him. His many awards have included 15 Grammys, 13 "Ebbys" (The Ebony Music Awards), four platinum albums, 17 gold singles. *Playboy* put him in The Playboy Music Hall of Fame in 1976 and compared him to another child prodigy: Mozart!

Los Angeles Mayor Tom Bradley proclaimed March 18, 1974, as Wonder Day. People like Barbra Streisand and Frank Sinatra have recorded his songs. Praise is heaped upon him.

But he remains the same, speaks haltingly, speaks admiringly about colleagues, emphasizes the comradeship in music (that made Paul Anka sing background vocals on one of Stevie's records).

"The world of music doesn't belong to any one person. All I do is my best," he says. "There's no number one, you know. If there were, number one should be pitied for number one wouldn't have anywhere to go."

The finest part of success to him is that he

receives love from those who hear him. The second best part is that he is able to immerse himself in sound, that he can afford to buy the most super-expensive recording equipment in existence and spend all his time enjoying and creating music.

That and his Yolanda and his child and his family and his friends – that's all he wants. His tastes are simple. His favorite drink is apple juice (he has his own apple juice maker). Hotels the world over offer him champagne and caviar, but he asks for chocolate chip cookies and hot tea.

The important thing is that he keeps going. He works on his unique voice every day, the way a virtuoso uses a violin.

That he spent three years creating *The Secret Life of Plants* and that some felt it was "too esoteric" or "too experimental" bothers him not. It was another step in his search for special truth. He was driven by a feeling that "there is a consciousness that binds all living things. I want people to look at the beauty that's right here on earth that we don't take time to see."

He knows the safe things to write about. Physical love, for instance. The pain of being left by a woman. He has written about that and will do so again. But this time, he wanted to say something else. So he did. In our over-commercialized world, it's like a breath of wintry air to come across something done for the love of it, a piece of art that's pure and free, no strings attached, an artist that says, "I did it because I like it."

Stevie's fans are a special kind of people. When he was scheduled to perform in New York for the first time in over two years recently, many of them camped overnight in front of the ticket office to be first in line. One young woman, 21, tells about it: "I've never done that before, not for anything or anyone. But Stevie . . . you know, there's no one like him. He's a big, big star, I know, but he's also *closer* to us than anyone else. The people there – they were fantastic. There was a feeling as if we all belonged to the same club. And we weren't all the same age or anything. There was a woman there who said she was 57 and a grandmother, and there was a skinny kid in eighth grade. We talked music and we talked Stevie. Someone said, 'When you're at his concerts, you don't feel like a customer, you feel more like a partner.' Or the grandmother-woman put it this way, 'I just love him! He isn't one of those who loves humanity but can't stand people!' When the ticket office opened, every ticket was sold within an hour. High prices but no regrets."

What now?

There have been rumors that Stevie "threatens" to record his next album at the Metropolitan Opera. Who knows?

A call to Motown: Do you know what Stevie's plans are? "You're kidding! He doesn't tell. Who knows?" Do you have any idea *when* we may expect his next record? *"You gotta be kidding!"*

But it'll come, and we can guess what it'll be about: love and lust and freedom and beauty and really *seeing*.

Meanwhile, Stevie sends everyone his message:

"You're a star, I'm a star. We'll shine forever if we just accept each other as we are."

**The true life story
of a man who sings of
love like no other**

BY EDDIE STONE

TEDDY PENDERGRASS

**WITH 16
PAGES OF
PHOTOS**

The years 1978-1979 were a rocket ship ride to the stars for Teddy Pendergrass. He came out of nowhere to hit the charts with million-seller albums and standing room only concerts, building a name that sent chills of excited passion up the spines of America's women. His was a meteoric rise unequaled in the annals of modern music history. ■ ■ ■ In a year, "Teddy Bear," as he is known to his legions of female fans, reached a pinnacle that most entertainers never attain during their lifetimes. The magic and the music were there, and Teddy was a star. ■ ■ ■ What Teddy has achieved in so short a time is a dream. He has become the epitome of the good life with his high media visibility accentuating his lifestyle. He has become a role model, not only to his peers, but to other, younger blacks who are looking for heroes. Teddy is a type, he's a different kind of entertainer who keeps it tasteful but sexy, who is able to make it all work—on stage and off.